Sounds the Living Make

Also by D. James Smith

Poetry
Prayers for the Dead Ventriloquist

Prose fiction
My Brother's Passion

Prose fiction, Young Adult
Fast Company
The Boys of San Joaquin
Probably the World's Best Story About a Dog and the Girl
Who Loved Me
It Was September When We Ran Away the First Time

Sounds the Living Make

Poems

D. JAMES SMITH

STEPHEN F. AUSTIN STATE UNIVERSITY PRESS
2012

Stephen F. Austin State University Press
P.O. Box 13007, SFA Station
Nacogdoches, TX   75962-3007
sfasu.edu/sfapress
sfapress@sfasu.edu

Cover photo: "Breaking Fog, Bridge Over San Joaquin" © Jim Curnyn
Author photo: Mindy Short

Manufactured in the United States of America

LIBRARY OF CONGRESS IN PUBLICATION DATA
Smith, D. James
Sounds the Living Make / D. James Smith

p. cm.
ISBN: 978-1-936205-77-6

1. Poetry. 2. American Poetry 3. D. James Smith

ACKNOWLEDGMENTS

I appreciate the editors and staffs of the following magazines in which these poems or versions of them first appeared:

Alaska Quarterly Review "Anima Mundi"
Blackbird "Turning"
Bald Ego "Easy," "That Year, A Novella," "Wilfred Owen"
Blue Mesa Review "Only In The Last Hour"
Borderlands: Texas Poetry Review "The Field," "There Comes A Day"
Carleton Arts Review "The Hidden Factor," "No Lesson"
Chattahoochee Review "Still in the River"
Chiron Review "In A Tidal Fumbling," "Ocean Song"
Confluence "After Good & Evil"
Cutbank "Miss Seibert"
Dalhousie Review "March Morning"
Epoch "The Last Days of Elvis"
Greensboro Review "A Living"
Green Mountains Review "A Thread"
Hayden's Ferry Review "Arthur on Leave from the Boys' Home Shows Me"
Laurel Review "Touchstone"
Malahat Review "The Strangers"
Margie "Rain"
New Delta Review "The Dreamers"
New Millennium Writings "The Peace"
New Orleans Review "Cold Blessing," "The Fall"
Nightsun "Red Is Always Twilight"
Nimrod "The Arrival," "Holiday," "Any Sunday"
Notre Dame Review "Legacy," "Now the Clouds Are Gone"
Passages North "I'd Go On," "The Widow"
Poetry Canada Review "Sunrise Meeting"
Poetry International "Possum"
Poet Lore "Every Fall is the Same"
Quarterly West "What I See From a Distance"
Southern Poetry Review "Note Without Flowers"
Spoon River Poetry Review "The Reconciliation"
Sundog: The Southeast Review "Figure in Midnight Blue"
The Sun "New Year's Day, Los Angeles"

Weber Studies "Fire," "The Wedding"
West Branch "Retreat"
Willow Springs "Man with Woman in Red."

"The Arrival" & "Anima Mundi" appeared also in the anthology *How Much Earth,* Heyday Books, 2001.

I am grateful to the National Endowment for the Arts for a grant which helped in the completion of these poems.

With special appreciation to the editor, Kimberly Verhines

Thank you to Michael Antrim, Linda Barron, Max Blagg, Michelle Bowden, Corrinne Clegg-Hales, Peter Everwine, Brenda Hillman, Sonya Janian, Philip Levine, Robert Pack, DeWayne Rail, Josephine Redlin, Mark Sanders, Gary Short, Roberta Spear, Linda St. John, Alfonso Velasco, & Julie Wilson.

CONTENTS

I.   *A Living*

Any Sunday   17
A Living   19
I'd Go On   20
Reading Wilfred Owen   21
A Thread   24
Every Fall, The Same   25
Legacy   26
The Field   28
Figure in Midnight Blue   30
Rain   31
There Comes A Day   33
The Hidden Factor   34
Anima Mundi   35
Fire   36
Red Is Always Twilight   38

II.   *The Arrival*

The Arrival   43
The Wedding   44
The Widow   45
March Morning   46
Man With Woman In Red   47
In A Tidal Fumbling   48
Now The Clouds Are Gone   49
Turning   51
The Strangers   53

Cold Blessing   56

Arthur on Furlough from the Boys' Home, Shows Me   58

The Fall   60

Miss Seibert   61

Still In The River   63

Sunrise Meeting   64

Possum   66

III.   *The Last Days of Elvis*

The Last Days of Elvis   69

No Lesson   70

Ocean Song   73

After Good and Evil   75

Retreat   77

What I See From a Distance   78

Only In The Last Hour   79

Holiday   81

The Dreamers   83

New Year's Day, Los Angeles   85

Note Without Flowers   86

Easy   88

The Reconciliation   90

That Year, A Novella   92

Touchstone   94

The Peace   95

For Kim

A Living

Any Sunday

I remember drinking
in the tired bar of a Times
          Square hotel, near the end
of a long, pathetic adolescence, vowing
art or suicide, thinking the little thistles
          of blood coughed in my handkerchief
a portent of some fatal beauty.
I admired the scarred and simple
          hands of the bartender, hollowing a perfect
gleam into the eyes of shot glasses,
stacked with the bleary, multitudinous
          light of votive candles,
the men who came and went,
their drinking, serious and quiet.
          When finally I dreamt
of fishing through the warped hardwood
floors of my rooms and hauled up
          a slick white egret, snagged in the neck
and hanging dead from my pole
like a delicate Chinese kite, I woke
          and left that city, sick with fear.

Yet, all my life I've gone on studying
the anonymous techniques of light, weaving
          the branches of a lamppost or the rainslicked
wheels of cars and trucks
or how silence follows a clap
          of gunfire from beneath the crosstown freeways—
even the occasional random tapping of hail
on an apartment roof at midnight.
          Out west the warm blonde hills roll,
swelling for miles toward the sea.
Any Sunday a man can get lost

driving out that unspoken restlessness
that rises and falls and tightens in the mind
like wind twirling in towers of dust
          sweeping the roadside. Sometimes, all it takes
is the furious smack of windshield wipers to startle me
enough so that I pull alongside a fruitstand
          or old roadhouse closed for years, the weather
bruised, low-bellied,
the birds winging by, alive,
          dark and close.

Once I stood at the edge of cliffs,
                    sea-lashed, crumbling, red, the cold
          blunting my senses, shouting
my doubt, wind-snatched so quickly
as to go unheard. And still I think
          we are so many lives arrived here
like insects carried on the wind,
miles past any wanting or design,
          the freeways' looping backward
curves emblematic of the haste
with which we circle
          out and back from selves
we sometimes hate.
Far overhead I watch
          the wedging gulls strung, fluttering
in evening air, their long kitetails
of light, ocean-bound, finally blown
          so high they resemble flecks
of salt—the heart's attachments, that secret
upward rushing, last of the sun
          burnishing the water's wind-tipped surface.

A Living

The wind's been brushing over the rise,
and through the heads of the sycamores
planted close to the fanged wire fence,
and coming down this way for the last hour
across the alkaline flat where I'm living
and sitting now on the porch, cheeks and ears stung
by cold, going numb in that same needling way
they warm when one grows slowly drunk.

Spring's about here; you can see it in the mossed
nubs of the trees' antlers, in the way the kids
nuzzle in clumps at the end of the day.
There's too much sky in this town, they told me when I started.
Last fall, the vines picked, their hands torn
and welted, they arrived in new clothes, called me sir,
wouldn't read without a threat, but liked the warmed room
well enough, stayed still like calves getting tender.

I know it's Billy Kessler that's got me out here.
He came in late again today, said he was up early
scrubbing a hog his dad had hung to drain.
I've told them my stories, even the secret psalms
that I shouldn't. I never knew how few sounds the living make.
When Alice-Marie threw herself into the river,
no one faulted her for the cliché she'd made of herself
coming up like that, bloated and pregnant.

I got shuddery that day, erasing the board, long past
what it needed, my thoughts, pencils flicked out a window;
no one tittered, not even a cough. The next morning,
there was a photograph on my desk, her standing
on the same sandy spot near the bridge where they found her,
hand just coming up to catch the hair blowing away
from her face, and Billy comes in, eyes flinty and strange,
gives me a ham wrapped in newspaper. And I stayed.

I'd Go On

Another dry year for the orchards.
When the heat sifts off, I walk

rinsed in moonlight, gentle with myself.
I know an underground lake rests beneath the valley,

a hundred thousand acres like pure wine asleep in darkness.
I remember, once, standing for hours in the dry cup

of a riverbed, humming to be heard, fingers of the wind
rushing over my face, my hair and my neck, my lantern

whipped down to a frail yellow leaf that flickered. Camped
on a bluff where wild burros stamped shy circles above us

my brother, silver pail for water in one hand,
tiny tab of acid in the other, had smiled

and walked out of the glow our fire etched in the desert.
That was but three years before he arrived in the belly

of a plane out of Asia; they gave my mother a flag
and my father little holes for eyes

like the ones I popped open with a .22
in the pomegranates, hung, stilled in their orbit.

If I were to lie down now I'm afraid
I'd branch down to the water. I'd hear the soft shuffle

of burros, solemn and holy, a twig cracking in the distance.
And I'd go on like this, singing him home, trying.

Reading Wilfred Owen

For comfort and finding none,
paper, thin as scripture,
   I look up
into the hard November starlight
bristling outside my window.

I know that light
doesn't stand for anything
    except the simple brilliance
that distance sucks into darkness.
    And yet, I love those generations

that made crude figures of them, patterns
to steer by.
    These terrible, glowing stanzas call
up the day gusts of rain
passed back and forth outside the plate glass

windows of White Front Department Store,
    a monolithic Quonset hut hulking
over the main strip of a city in California
that decayed before it came to anything,
    and where I worked, cynical and knowing

nothing but an adolescent, tidal fumbling
    toward some television hack's
notion of manhood. My dad,
who always took
strength from anger, this time

looking frail and hopelessly
fragile in a cheap transparent raincoat,
    pulled up in a Yellow Cab, that

so extravagant I knew.
                    But, his eyes, shot

with flecks of pencil-lead and crimson,
mouth, crumpled at the corners, hot with brandy
went on about it anyway, what Khe Sahn was
and how my brother had lain down
                    somewhere I'd never see.

Late, nights like this, moon-driven and nicotined,
                    the river smoking fog
            over the fields, I see
                    the eyes of feral cats sparking in the grass.
Spun by instinct they twist,

rear up as if to strike,
            then crouch back
                    mewling at one another,
making the sound of human babies.
Sometimes, disturbed by that fray,

I go outside to lay down a little
fire with the .22 he left behind,
            the last evidence
of his ever having been.
            But I do not forget

that he is nothing
more than the abrupt silence
that follows those pre-dawn dancers
leaping off into thick leaves
            of night. Then, beneath the stars,

I have the privacy I thought I wanted
            and can't love anymore.
Sometimes, I like to think
                    a ladder of light
could swing low enough for me,

and my hands go up,
involuntarily,
        as tiny chains of quick, red coals
break and flare, seeding the dark,
                scattering, dead.

A Thread

A yellow leaf caught on the end
of a spider's thread
spins, a lure.

It holds me attached to this day.
I can feel rain tensing in the clouds,
moving like dark freighters.

Sometimes, on afternoons like this,
you can watch sand cranes
working their way south toward Paraguay.

There is a map in their heads
extending itself, a light stretched
along the bones in their necks.

There are these leaves
spinning in the wind
and lightning arcs

across the sky's brain-gray.
Somewhere above a field
at the bottom of the world,

in the center of the picture
in your mind now, there are
birds opening like parasols.

Every Fall the Same

The green goes in September,
and the great mulberry scaffolding above

my father's yard still holds
the presence of my brother;

where he once climbed, quills
of light plunge solid darkness

to touch ground
that the overgrown leaf-shag

of limbs grazes gently in places.
It's a thing so simple and whole

he'd like it—winding with sap
through the waist of the trunk,

out finally to the tips that leaf
and let go. Wasn't he

blown skyward in pieces,
perhaps the size of these leaves,

so suddenly, he and I still need this
slow drifting down through the years?

In the evenings, feeding blackbirds return
like the lovers he never married

and now in his age no longer fears.
They chatter and weave through the branches,

leap and sing in close to the center.

Legacy

Uncle on the bed, oval of lamplight
        grazing his shoulder. I know he's awake,
because I'm seven, bright, already saddling

        the mares of my imagination. I like
the tin horse on the nightstand.
        I like when he coughs that his chest rattles—

a leather bag of marbles,
        the way he winks without meaning to
when he talks. He's given me a taste of a Lucky non-filter,

        two fingers of milk in a glass tumbler to see
me through stories of Berlin, the war,

        the farm gone bust in Nebraska, shrunk
now to a spoonful of bourbon
        the bottle, without a ship, has tipped on the floor.

        Morning edges the windows then blossoms
an unintelligible pink on the wall,

        and I know what *black sheep* means,

and I know of the ladies he falls for—*like a fool*—
        in saloons that leave his eyes polished

and still. I know I could go into that distance
        just by sitting in the closet, holding my breath
until stars spill like confetti and I awaken face down

        in a ruin of shoes. Already I'm worried about the future.
That dark angel who quashes my sleep

has peed my side of the bed again,

and when father comes to get me,
polished brogues, white shirt
    pressed crisp in submission,

he'll hide his shame and his disapproval
    in the arch of the doorway,
and nobody's eyes will ever meet, though we were

    just lambs, then, and tired and so lying down.

The Field

The pumps push water,
white moonlight riding its back,
down the long rows of vines
staked out and twisted,
slugs swelling like black lips from the stems.
Hours ago you watched
                    dusk flying in its innumerable dots,
packed tight as a sunflower's center.
Sometimes memory is a bird's cry
                    dropped, cold,
through sky brushed lemon and blue,
            a dog's lonely bark.

Was it a woodpecker? the one
with a corn-red throat and flecked wings,
            flushing so quickly
that as a child, you could just catch it
                    out of the corner of your eye.
And leaf-shadow and wind
making the wrought iron fences
            ripple and kneel down.
Then, in the evenings, no one but you
believed the blind madness
that lighted dull moths
            in the lantern of grandfather's head,
the works inside nibbled down
until they found him one morning
                    weeping, naked under an elm.

The soil cupped in your hands,
                    trails out in the wind,
east where light follows
the cracked spine of the Sierras,

You spin toward heaven,
the drone of two sudden cropdusters
come thrashing low
over the ridge,
black bellies just clearing the lines,
        and you bow, welcome what dawns.

Morning, you cross back
                over the field to your father's house,
patched over with ivy, porch-sagged,
                wind-tattered, rain-blown with years,
a sack of swallows
bulbing like a goiter
from the eaves, and two black bricks
        missing from the mouth of the chimney top.
        But, the mulberry, still muscular
leafs out over the rooftop,
and in the oat grass a rusted bell
        that once announced Amos—goat, friend,
advisor to children and old men.

Sun dumped on the back stoop,
made of smooth polished river rock,
                roots you there, timeless,
absent, the windmill in the yard
creaking ceaselessly
like a love that follows you,
loving you too much,
        your body filled with its sounds
so that you see walking,
out of a field gone to fire,
a figure, half-smiling, waving,
then withering in sunlight.
                And the leaves coming down
like small birds to your hands.

Figure in Midnight Blue

At dusk sun drags its sleds of light
　　over the horizon, tall shadows
of monkey puzzles, tethered in windbreaks,
　　beginning their slow trot across the fields,
plowed black and waiting.
　　When the long fingers of water
come crawling the rows,
　　they are as blue as moonlight. *This is it.*

My wife kicks the pickup door open
　　to coil in the doorjamb, charcoal to sketchpad,
rasping a quick even stroke.
　　I close my eyes and settle in. Time wavers—
wind through the ditch grass, ruffling.
　　Her sounds take me back
to the first time I felt truly naked,
　　standing in an upstairs room

while the afternoon sun
　　made a halting pilgrimage across the floorboards,
and I listened to her breath, torn,
　　circling in swift migration
as she lay down her brush and reached out,
　　fingertips grazing the line of my back.
Late, that night, I watched
　　when she rose, gathering herself

in a red, woolen blanket, her small
　　pots of oil, spread about her in the dark,
shining like the eyes of children. She showed me,
　　then, how to lift out of this world
its divisions: the cheek's sharp escarpment,
　　the delicate shells of the ears, beads
of salt and light that can travel the lips,
　　the body that had been mine, made whole.

Rain

If you walked out
of a rented room
tucked under pines
where the road climbs one last
hill before plunging to the graying
blonde sands of the Pacific
and saw four deer standing
in a rain-swept
parking lot looking
as if they'd been waiting all night
for you, you might think
of the white crane that came
to talk to you as a child
the night after your uncle stepped
backward into the spinning
prop of a cropduster
he was gassing.
Then he was just sky
changing color, your brother said,
though you could only imagine
him there and then not,
and the crane said that
was alright. You might see
in the frank appraisal
of their great blinking eyes
the little pools shining
from your father's face
after the morphine kicked
into him like an idiot
mule, so much
like the profound, dark,
anonymous rain
that gathers in the holes of stones
in the fields beyond the borders
of the city you grew up in.

You'd see they are confused
but want something from you,
and fear tethers them, staring,
as if you held an answer.
So you would marvel
at the hard glassy hooves
that could slash you reflexively
and without remorse,
but on which one now steps
tentatively forward, muscles
tensing in the haunches
of his brothers. And you
know that any move
would be reckless, any
hope of a blessing foolish,
yet you say in a rash whisper
what you should have then.
Say, *It's alright,*
before their bodies
become water, the rain
blown suddenly sideways,
away from you.

There Comes a Day

When the heart tightens,
the tiny bolts snugged into place,

a child pulling away from the window
and that cold light stacked

like kindling on a wooden porch.
No one's left then to listen

when the doves break from the palms
with the sounds of soft applause.

No one loves their little shoulders.
No one hunts the moon anymore.

No one pays the old women to weep.
When it happens it's like someone

placing tickets to the theater
into the bottom of a drawer.

On the dresser, a blue pebble
kept for a long time.

This faint odor of rain,
and winter dusk, quickening.

Somewhere there must be lovers turning
away in their sleep. Somewhere

on a corner, the wind slows and eddies,
picks up bits of paper and runs on.

Somewhere a dog lopes
past houses it doesn't recognize.

The Hidden Factor

I never remember robins moving in flocks
until I see them sweep into a stand of apples
and quiver there, chests of soft suede.

The wind kicks up; the branches twist;
the creatures lift and dip, banking hard
off morning's cuff. Once, my grandfather

lifted me over his head into a soft-water day
like this. I stood on the palms of his hands
to touch the fruit he meant for me:

peaches, figs—cuttings from the old country,
loved here into bloom. Many times
I make a connection between

the look or the sound of a thing
and the meaning of another.
And though I know it's more than science

or superstition, I make too much of it.
Like this sun that's worming
down now in little flecks of light

making me wish the robins hadn't fled or that grandfather
could still make that whistling in his teeth
when he laughed and the birds took off.

Anima Mundi

In the rain clouds that fountain the horizon,
      in the silver leaves of the birches
flashing and turning like minnows,
      in the wind-flattened grass and wild roses,
something rises—even in the sleepy crowns of blued slugs
      pouring slowly from knotholes in the fence,
or this morning the way that black scavenger you watched
      snapped wide the pleated fans of its wings
and with all the sullen witchery of its kind
      glided down the glassy heat
shaking over a filed of sunflowers.
      Whatever it is is worth loving,
though it does not regard you in any way;
      it slips like the dusk flooding from the trees
as you turn toward those shadows
      that oil the ditchbanks and the swallows
that fold now in darkness.

Fire

Late spring in the valley
and the wing-whistle of dove
is constant as they rise
and fall from the trees, foraging
      for seed the wind brings.
On the ground they blur with rotted bark
until they move, and
the earth seems to crawl. Kimberly loves them and points
to starlings far above, black drops
in a blue pool—mixing, swirling,

some bleeding off, some left, tightening their circle,
      wound higher and higher.
How far light has to travel, she says. And, of course, then I see it
firing the bushes, dousing the crape myrtles in silver.
I remember, once, quieted, we watched,
across a river, an ancient eucalyptus,
white, tall as a god,
      in the heat somehow ignited,
columns of smoke streaming skyward,
      before it exploded, black rolling from its top

like huge barrels of oil, the limbs crackling down,
falling, opening, red as the interior of bones.
We stayed until it was over, just coals stirring,
black-backed with underbellies flaring,
wind-traced in lines.
That summer she'd brought a boy home
      from the ward,
his skin stung, stripped by flame. Blotched
with the face of a calf, he wobbled around the yard
all of an afternoon—stunned

with what was once familiar, fresh textures, soil,
the sticky leaves of oleanders—afraid of the sun,
the odds, three to one he'd die of infection.
And she who is good
        said, *Still, I've never believed in evil.*
            God, what would that be like to wake,
wings of heat waving from your shoulders,
arms like wicks, too soft
to swim out
from those bright sheets of fire?

            I've never trusted
these days that languish & close,
                    sudden as a candle thumbed out
in the distance, woolen darkness sweeping overhead.
   Lord, what are the odds I'd ever come to you,
except as a child, taking a chance,
            running outside some desperate night
to find myself, alone, beneath stars,
all those little deaths,
brilliant with their burning.

Red is Always Twilight

Sitting again, hours at a stretch, while my brother squints,
        jabbing at the canvas where
my face begins to sprout in shades of persimmon and milk,
          I'd like to know
how I first awaken in his mind before the lines arrive
            to arrange themselves.
The sliding door is open, and outside, sun flecks a pair
            of wooden chairs
slathered in whitewash. This afternoon, I listened absently
            to faint plosives of rain
opening on the rooftop, his brush scratching dry muslin as he
            explained his theory
of color. Myself, I think red is always twilight—embers that
            crumble, winter coming on
in black silhouettes. Or I will look at yellow and still,
            sometimes, see Peter's hair: bright
reedy clumps that came away in his mother's hand when she'd
            pet him—13, brain mushrooming
tumors the size of thumbs, pushing his eyes finally blind.
            I remember he'd fight
sleep unless the drapes were open and his box of sky there.
            Boys, we three
talked of lights in his forehead then as glass tubes of an old radio
            that pulsed and crackled faintly
until they sipped a whole darkness. After that my brother
            never had a friend. And I
have felt a certain swift and painful shyness overcome me when
            I love another creature. I suppose
blue is just the hard mothering of atmosphere and light
            falling into every day without question.
It's out there now, beyond the peak of the house, behind my
            brother's head, swirling with the clatter of pigeons
circling, there in the coming dusk, the one fat palm that fronts

the property. I'd want the true
plum-green shimmer of their smooth Victorian bellies
        somewhere in the work I'd do, if
what I made were pictures. I'd paint a white star in the corner
        of my brother's eye, a tiny spot that pulls
the full spectrum in and gives it back, the furious silent desire
        that's in all things before they calm and pass.

The Arrival

The Arrival

After rain, clean watercolor light.
The young grass, jumped-up in gravel
along the tracks, is plush, avocado green.
Last night the rush of a train's
metallic shuffle, the long, delicious
question of its horn, was heart music,
ordinary and true. I listened while
moths thrummed themselves, crippled,
at the screened window
until sleep made the bed sheets over
into wet wings wrapped round my body.
Now somebody across the river
has an oil drum going, smoke rolling off,
hanging in daybreak like swarms of bees.
Light, clarified by long illness,
I have finally stopped expecting
the future to be that good day
we all want to walk into.
And what I have, which is nothing
more or less than this one cloud
suffused with desert red, stilled overhead,
or the phlox that flames the rusting cattle gate,
I save for you. Even this tern
struggling to lift above the stubble
daubed in below oak and sycamore
seems as necessary as you, your tiny figure
waving from the house, salt-white, set back
in gray tress, the rippling shape
of my shadow leading me
across the meadow like a friend.

The Wedding

All day tassels of wheat burn
in the field where crows rise,
      flagging their hunger and contempt,
waving off in pure sunlight.
      Muscles throbbing, bathed and cool,
I lie down to watch you sleep.
      I know my word has turned your heart
the way water does a wheel
      for you sag against me, light,
your ribs, hollow flutes.
      Somewhere a god must have played her song,
and I listened
      and fell to earth—soil, work,
this bed, a leaf swirling
      and the water running home.
I pitch my ear to the course
      of that current, a voice thickly rich,
and go down on ropes of air
      past fishes, slow zeppelins
that whir when they rise then drift
      to rest on the bottom.
The heart, too, is a creature that feeds
      and kicks in its nest of blood.
How shy and rocking
      in its perfect motion.
You said if something
      were to happen to me,
you'd have little except, sometimes,
      maybe, a presence in the room.
Sometime, that will happen to one of us.
      Love, I think, *love,* placing my ear
to your chest, *that one could always remember*
      this sounding deep,
and the words for it.

The Widow

Across the meadow, bright in a box the window makes,
my neighbor, old widow, sits sewing what I know
are monograms of crimson, pushed through the stiff
cuff of a dead man's shirt. Late afternoon and
seagulls list inland glazed with the last light,
wings bent like boomerangs, pulling a dusk
of blue-black and lavender. I go on scribbling
with this steady care that is itself a kind of sewing
oneself into the pages of being, stilled, in the presence
of what remains untouched and troubling

because it seems to seek a name.
The pines have strewn their thwarted passion
in cones of rust along the lane that is brittle
with winter and smells fine—oil and dust.
I guess, I want it all. Though a teacher once
told me the task was to let desire
go of neglect. Our neighbor has said
she enjoys watching us, my wife and me,
and come Christmas slipped a card under the door.
Etched simply into the wrinkled blue

expanse of an expensive paper in rich and trembling
black: *Love—spend all.*
Yes. Doesn't the heart, that great loom, want,
always something, shuddering up and clacking
when I see, say, this sliver of moon
rafting the surface of my eyes, or, now,
the irrefutable specific of my love approaching
up the long drive, orchids of breath pushed
before her in the cold, evening stitched tight
to the shoulders of her coat of brilliant red.

March Morning

In the stupor of rising, half-wakened,
I walked out to the first leaves
shot out of the branches like hands
in a soundless birthing cry.

Blinking I stared. Car-killed, mashed,
with the sun still in its eye, hung
in the mouth of my constant shepherd
was the orange, nameless cat

brought here last summer when
mouse droppings peppered my doorstep.
If you've ever felt a dog-toy to any man
you'll know why I pressed

the animal's soft lips
against its certain teeth
to force the jaw to let go its gift
and laid that cat out straight-away

in an earth-wrenched church
of weeds and rotted bark.
Still wild with light
rushing from its eyes,

limbs stiffening past rest,
it was caught, paw-bent,
in a leap it couldn't finish.
It was spring, and the day

still a whole long dream
before me, and already
my black-saddled dog
beginning to whimper, to dig.

Man with Woman in Red

A sliver of moon beginning to fade
as a starling traces its quick calligraphy
          across my window. Then the first human
movement as my neighbor turns
his wheelchair half-circle on the porch of his trailer,
cups his ear and listens toward the east.

          When the girl comes, so young I wonder
what he's paying, she opens the red wings
of her raincoat to hug him, and he clings to her
so that for a moment they look like birds, feeding.

It's not hard to understand he once said, losing
your balance like that; it's like falling
in love and no one catching you
or taking you into their arms.

It was six years ago while waiting
for a train that his legs, as if longing
to climb into a grave, stepped
          off an elevated platform. He told me

when the others started jumping after him
to pull what was left of him off of the tracks
he thought they were angels descending

          crying, *Oh, god, man*, dragging
him by the coat, all of them wailing,
kneeling in the gravel, their hands
dipped the color that has always
signified love.

In a Tidal Fumbling

Mid-twenties, married, she's pretty
with eyelashes that remind me
of blackened monarchs I've torn
from the quivering edges of leaves.
I'm seventeen. I ask her to touch
herself. She says she can't, unless
she were made to. *I'm making you,*
I say. So an early afternoon, sieved-in
through curtains of muslin, is tangerine,
and I'm a quiet monk, coiled, supplicant,
at the foot of the bed, the bed
a pool of warm water with flowers
that float over the surface, ripple
and open. Triangles of light gather
in the mirror, spill into the corner.
My chest fills like a paper lantern, lifts
and sways, bumping the ceiling where
I rock in smoke curling from a candle.
Her fingers are long and tapered;
the red nails flicker. They smell of rosemary
and soil. With the pleasure of breaking
a small law, her voice, a wood rasp,
she shudders and says, *You're not making
me do this.* But I know that.
I've already passed out
of myself two or three times
and am having trouble
getting back into my legs.
I don't want to be a shadow
anymore. I don't want this loneliness,
the empty rushing. I'm still a boy,
I want a body
I can govern.

Now the Clouds are Gone

        though wind still moves the trees
where small leaves, unfolding,
net the moon, back of it, stars treading black water.
I am dumb beneath that bright constancy, in a way
I used to go when you undressed, standing at the windows,
trembling, a sparrow my voice couldn't calm,
            so that when we would lie, finally, down
            I could feel you beating about
somewhere above us, thrashing the ceiling.

One day you said
you believed books were the coffins of dead men's minds
            and refused to see me anymore.
I wanted you to understand that it was worth wanting
what we'll never have—all the names I promised you,
            the trees in the city struck red
come April, the apartment walls sloshed
with shadows tugging evening
            and the white paper glowing...

I remember one spring we hiked
that sand trail edging a creek. The snow-melt
            was running early, the first grass
dumped with flowers—popcorn, butterweed,
even the little bonnets
of some stickseed showing, the breeze sifting
down soft as grace. The dark pennies of your
breasts pressed your blouse, your rabbit's eyes
            opening petals of light in my head.

                            Somewhere
there was the stinging infant cry of feral cats, the quick
            swart birds rustling brush, darting

clear, twining air. And then a kind of sleep, something old
and ongoing—until I stood and saw again
how each thing streamed
          into the world, to spend itself,
without measure, not named or stilled, not signified,
not mine to hold.

Turning

You never flinch when we lie down, your eyes on mine,
step for step in the way figure skaters couple, glide and
dip. When I look too long into the dark I see how desire
swells in the mind in a long fomenting ache, leaning
toward what it thinks is its moment of transcendence
until it's poured back and pestled down in the frail vessel
of the body. You want it that way, the empty stairway
on the ward where you work and that you insist we climb,
where a gallery of pigeons pace their awkward nests
in the opened skylight hanging over us, their gurgled coos
and clattering rush battering the shaft of light that pins us
there, pulsing like huge monarchs, our wings unfurled.
You throw the future out onto the bald carpet of our room;
again and again the coins reveal: *Revolution.*
When I touch you, the irises of your eyes begin to float
up like small planets, though you still come, hard,
down that slow river of stars, skin stretched tight
over the raft of your collarbones, your hips a reflexive cough.
You start lunching with a surgeon. He has small, hesitant
teeth and fine shirts and you say he talks of the difficulties
of opening bodies, separating the lungs from the heart.
Kidneys that are like purses hard with jewels, livers slapped
quivering into steel pans, almost the size of small babies.
Together you walk the lawns at work, feed the half-tamed
crows and the many starlings that fill the sky, black scratches
on a bright mirror... I can't stop myself from watching.
I sell my back as day labor, drive out the long wound
of highway laid down across the coastal range to lose myself
in the small clear bowl of a valley there, chopping out the old
orchards planted a century ago. One night in November I lie
in a hick-town hospital, my shoulder rearranged when a branch
I'd straddled whipped and bucked with the force of a bull.
Stupid, slack-jawed, slathered in my own saliva and

doused with enough morphine to swim off down the hall
nosing the walls, I study the bad landscapes there—
dogwoods snowing over a riverbank, the liquid yellow grass
sprung through the Gothic ribs of rotting boats, then you—
just outside the window—coming for me, eyes on mine,
your nurse-whites unbuttoned, that black hair of yours
streaming out behind you, unwoven, wild,
that host of ravens at your back.

The Strangers

Slipping over the ribbon of asphalt
that spools around the rough side of Table Mountain
and forks sharply off 41
to follow a stream that miners once panned,
I was, then, poor and a little angry, and thinking,
foolishly, I had something coming.
Where twilight touched the grass and darkness sailed
past me, the fence posts, the cutting, invisible wires,
I'd pull up the gravel trail slowly, bearing
west through the nameless pastures of youth,
hands faintly lit by my bike's speedometer.
I'd scent through my helmet the acrid
scat of squirrels and coyotes, cool grasses,
and pulled by an animal longing, sometimes,
catch an owl veering noiselessly
through the wobbly cone of my headlight.
I'd coast to a stop and leave
the bike nosed into a bank of manzanita,
the engine ticking quickly,
and take the last rise on foot.
Braver than I and strange,
she lived in a tent
similar to those you might find in Tibet,
large, rounded, the black smoking pipe of a chimney
poked up through its center.
She'd pull back the flap of the door and greet me,
a half-smile playing over her face
when she'd see the carton of Salems
I would have stolen from the market where I worked
for tuition I never saved because
they paid three twenty-two an hour
and in nineteen seventy-four
my only true ambition

was to own a gentleman's Norton Commando,
that, and to follow the bright,
crimped threads in the books I could have
for nothing at the public library.
This isn't a parable of loss.
She never loved me and, truly,
I don't recall her name.
It's got more to do with trying
to map a way back
through the ordered monotony of days
I have constructed around me
to a woman who taught me proper fear.
She was like that something that once brushed
over me in the dark when I camped
alone one summer in southern Oregon.
Whatever it was woke me, and I would have run away,
though didn't because there was no moon
and many places I might fall.
She'd lie there, moving beneath me in silence,
and I would sense I was struggling
over the surface of a deep, secretive lake
in which one might drown
and some surely have. That's mythical;
I should have known that
from the silver anklets she wore
like a god out of the east,
the vague manner of her eyes appraising me,
hands cupping my cheeks, her hair
curled with incense. I want to be
plainspoken, and you can go with me
this little ways, if you choose,
up the road to a lighted tent
still glowing some thirty years later,
and see, again, that it's true, that sometimes
we draw close enough to that anonymous other
that we feel the huge mystery and awe,

especially if you're nineteen,
and the woman lives alone and doesn't need you
as you once imagined the world needs you.
She has hair, shining rich and coarse
as the feathers of ravens;
the strong supple curves of her hips
take the shape of you, exactly,
and you'll have what you wanted and more,
to go all the way, to sink with no name
like water poured down into water.

Cold Blessing

Trembling as if gut-shot, I sit
with a priest, a stranger, an alcoholic I think,
his face, quiet as a burned field.
He says, *Remember yourself as a child?*
I nod, see my old Columbia bicycle
saddled with news of the world
on a morning so cold my hands were blue,
and I, lord
of the black streets, struggling
deep into the heart of that city.

Well, after death all this will be like that, vague,
unimportant, a memory that slips by and you say,
'Oh, I remember that.'
Later, awake in the darkness, a siren
echoing in the street, I think, Oh *that.* Suffering.

Father, the spine in the neck of my friend
was whittled down to the finest necklace of pain,
the morphine no help.
He rigged himself to the wench of his jeep.
You understand. A man of great intention and faith,

he sat down in a chair out behind his place
where he could see the tree line begin
and wound his throat closed
with a thin nylon strap.
The oaks remain, sheets of light
driving out of the south,
the birds coming in, snippets
of rags dropped in the branches.
A picture I might have drawn as a child.

Now, Father, I lie still
behind the twin shrouds of my eyes
and try to believe the little psalms
the air leaves in my ear.
That he would remember

skirting Bear Lake,
clouds of mist in the late afternoon,
night drifting up slowly behind us.
The fine drumming of rain on the leaves.
That. *That.*

Arthur on Furlough from
the Boys' Home Shows Me

Day breaks as the sun pulls
its swords from the earth.

I'm driving Arthur around.
It's what he chooses, though
he won't speak; he points:

telephone poles in the distance,
a smattering of small nameless birds
drifting across the sky.
He smiles,

shyly, his eyes, two drops
of black oil,
crowned with splinters
of gray. The police said
they found him, standing,

naked in the tub,
wet spiders of blood,
dangling from his mouth.

Arthur tries,
to chew his medication,
all at once. Saves it up,
under the tongue,

refusing the nurse's fingers,
the little bottles of water,
blue submarines
lining the night windows,

a marine darkness.
Nurse took his sweaty pulse;

later he took his own,
whispered he could feel the quick
fish slipping through.

He makes a house of paper,

puts the red crayons in,
grinds it slowly with his palms,

shakes the colors loose,

building a fire on his pillow.
We're just gliding now,

       Arthur and I,
to park beneath the huge
dark oak he's spotted, its trunk

flowing up out of this world

in thick brown waves
that pile and split into
their long solitary climbs.

We sit; he puts his hands
against the glass, fingers mimicking
the slight sway of branches.

I roll the windows down.
We listen for leaves,
brushing the silence.

His eyes are soft leaves.

He takes his pulse.

His eyes are water.

The Fall

Much is the good in my yard,
the squirrel dangling upside
down from an almond branch, rolling
his find in claws like an otter, the cat
teasing the smoke of its tail
along the weathered struts of the fence,
the one woodpecker who comes rarely
to fluff a fat, speckled chest
in the dog's water dish. Sometimes,
the pleasure of light falling
softly through leaves
is the resurrection, and then
how the flesh brims.
The snails, little caravans
loaded with Jesus,
push east. I almost believe that
when the right word chooses us,
we are not thinking at all
of ourselves,
and the arch of the garden gate,
the porous grain of the wood
that I touch roughly,
is in every part
constructed of love.
But, then something like
this scent of dead brambles,
recalls me and the violence
of moving that name, measuring
the weight of it, as if hand to hand,
Bramble, bramble, is the true fall.
And again the chaste patience begins.
pray for luck, I say, and the little mercies
of these birds darting clear
from the trees, this time yellow warblers,
flickering up and down quickly
as they gather themselves,
brief whispers, gone.

Miss Siebert

Some said she only stumbled
        or, she was having a fit. She did
totter there for a moment, the class
        going quiet, wondering
if it was for effect. But then she started up
        again as tiny lights under glass
of a pinball machine will whir on slowly,
        my teacher, though I did not know it then,

beautiful in her desolation, in a print dress
        matching the liver spots
flecked over her arms, somehow, still alive
        in the midst of our savagery and boredom.
Some said her mind seized, the way an engine
        clenches at its heart,
but it was arcing, electric, clearly there was
        movement, her limbs fluttering, her eyes

reaching back. *As a young woman,* she says, stops
        and stares at Jerry Zuniga, his huge half-back frame
folded into a desk, as if she knew his face
        would collapse inward that spring
like a rotted pumpkin—leukemia:
        a word that was opening before us like a flower—
her lips trembling, the petals of a flower
        battered by rain. *Deep,* she stutters,

in the down-hung apple branches
        dusk gathered. Swallows came clustering like bees.
We think it's all right. Jesus, it's one of her poems
        or another hard luck story. And she whirls
around once, as if looking for something
        lost. *The sun*
going where it must, she says, speaking again
        before sprawling

across the green and white checkered linoleum,
        the ambulance people and the principal,
in his worried brown suit
        and his brogues of authority, shouting
us out of the room, some of the girls
        refusing, some crying,
all of us gawking
        though not caring much.

We were there, she breathes. *Oh, it was sometime*
        during the depression, the men gone,
and the women.
        Oh god, can you imagine us,
skirts full of fruit, quiet
        by the river, those leaves
scattered over the surface, swirled and
        glinting in sunlight.

Still in the River

A rustle of rain in the trees
    will bring him back
where I can see him, working the far bank,
    clenching a pipe in corn-colored teeth,
face wrapped in dusk-light and smoke.
    My father liked the cold, solitary
trout that muscled off the bottom
    in the faint starlight that fades
just before dawn. I'd follow him there,
    and he, always a little surprised
I'd arrived. Once, with a candor I mistook
    for cruelty, he said to his river as
much as to me, *Marry young, and you'll regret it.*
    This isn't exactly like caring; it's more
a fascination skirring blind over a river, a desire
    for the hidden bright moment when
something inexplicably wild might beat again
    in my hands. A fish shucks its last light
the way in a dark room, a woman I knew shed
    a speckled evening gown. I can
hold it, vibrant and small and also
    enormous with something of what
I felt the one time he carried me,
    down the trail, on his shoulders.
Tonight I know the mind is going
    its own way, crawling like this cricket,
rain-soaked and trying to drag over my palm
    the hook I've pushed through its forehead
and thorax. Tonight, I'll make it walk on water,
    flicked back and forth over the surface,
the shadows of owls sliding through
    stands of white maple, glittering in moonlight.
The wind starts. A scuffling in the grass. Breathe,
    I say, breathe, and we begin.

Sunrise Meeting

It was before schooling or religion,
        before the blissful sensations of childhood
were given over to the Sisters of Mercy
        with their blessed candles and grammar.
It was in the 5 a.m. hush of any Sunday in winter
        before light in the east seared the Sierras, tribes
of starlings still nosing the wet lawns and roses.
        I'm sleepy, trying to keep my head from rolling
from my shoulders while Dad drives and whistles

in that, vague, distracted way of his.
        We're taking my grandfather
to the Southern Baptist Church Sunrise Meeting.
        And I wonder if my father likes his father
because anytime he's mentioned he shakes
        his head and clears his throat as if something's caught
there and worries him in a way he doesn't understand.
        I know he didn't read the good book grandfather dozed
over in the back seat. He believed in work,

the way it empties a man, leaves him simple
        and spent, too tired to think.
It's all been said, he once told me. So he was a disciple
        of silence, though fond of whistling
in that private way of his, and this day he surprises
        me, says, *Dad? You OK?* And Grandfather opens one eye,
waving him off with the leisure of age.
        Oh, the streets are brittle and shining, and I'm
calling out, *Right turn. This way,* taking care of them,

keeping that quiet, palpable
        as cotton, from filling the car and smothering
us. My father wouldn't care that I'm trying now,

with everything that I have, to keep him alive.
He wouldn't see the point. He's looking past me,
    watery gray eyes following Grandfather
stepping unsteadily up the walkway in his dark
    coat and shoes that are shining, towards the door
that would take him with something as certain as grace or love.

Possum

Terror of mice, distrusted and brooding,
unwilling to bother to hide himself
in the half-dark settling over the yard,
he'll stop, and clutching the fence top
with the cracked leather gloves of his hands,
suck air through his teeth at the sight of me.
Thin, tattered in the costume
of an alcoholic clown, he can't sit out the winter.
His is a lean anger, so much so I believe
that some evening should a fleck of grease travel
up into my brain, and, I, to die in the wet grass
under the cold insistence of stars,
he'd chew a hole, perhaps
in the soft fleshy spot under an armpit
and munch his good fortune with proper simplicity.
Sated, he'd sleep then with no dream of heaven.
Denied the lamb's bleating heart, he perfects solitude,
licks back the grief of the spleen and likes it.
Crazed with the stink of suburbs,
he hangs on and cares nothing for my admiration.
Sometimes at night, head tipped back on the sofa,
music coming to its expected end,
a velvet quiet bearing hard toward the center of things,
I think of him out there, snout low and scenting
for garbage or the stiff little carcass of a sparrow.
I go to bed and dream my dream,
the one where they cut my hair and clip my nails,
dress me in a silken box, arranging my head
to face the east and the little hole of silence
they say is a star.

The Last Days of Elvis

The Last Days of Elvis

Strung up in intensive care, seventh surgery in seven years,
I think of him near the end, how he was said to have lain

down, once, on his back, center stage in Las Vegas, singing softly
as though to himself, giggling where the refrain should've been,
and they loving him anyway, for his genius, for his excess, every

hillbilly's dream of sudden royalty. The best years of my life
were the times I abandoned myself to appetite

and ambition and suffered, and it's strange to know that, and this
drug after years of soft refusal feels exactly like love
washing over me in waves of insistent applause, my mind

a hand limply slung from the bed, dragged
deeply in the sewers of heaven, bones of the fingers

sucked clean by fishes. And the chorus girls' voices
swelling from the radio are his angels that I
don't need anymore...just this doctor's synthetic affection,

consciousness whip-flicked and guttering. I pass easily
in and out of mansions that I once only drove past in darkness.

I know I read somewhere that the self is a coffin, but it feels
like a drowned lover, sagging sodden against me. I thumb
the eyes closed, gently pet the wet head. Oh, Elvis, the girls

are going down on their knees and the house lights are rising,
and the doctor, hustled in through the stage door

off a sun-blasted alley, is thinking today he was to go flying,
and his mistress will be alone, watching old movies
and weeping. Oh, in the desert, all the time, every order of god is passing.

No Lesson

When you're sick, the waking
can be worse than when you go down
into the old basements of sleep,
ten hours or more, choking,
body smoked,
like a limb of green cedar.

I learned last Christmas,
the father of one
of the kids in my classes—
how many times have I heard
this?—puts his fingers
inside her. Her skin,
birch trees in winter,
a laugh that cuts you,
wet eyes like salt-
dipped olives. She's into
the Bible. *The Lord,*
He slew me.
I say, *I don't really understand.*
But, I see
the doves in her blouse.

I stand up and shuffle
from one foot to the next.
I say, *Love.* I say, *The meek*
shall inherit—maybe they're thinking,
vet, some kind of Vietnam
syndrome, my hands
shaking.

I drive by the liquor store,
neon rippling out into the dark

over Palm Avenue,
and see her climbing into a van.
Her mother is driving,
a milky face,

stars clipped

to her hair.
At the stoplight
they don't know me.
There are feathers of fog
in the air. It's December.

When, finally, I sleep,

the birds,
snug deep into my throat.

It's getting harder to breathe.
Doctors put a little pipe
in my neck.

I can't explain it. The children giggle.
Do you smoke? They want to know.
Lao Tzu says
suffering is the ordinary
means of transformation.
I say, *Smoke is the first evidence
of absence.*

She stares out the window
through the colored letters
and the black butterflies,
watches the wind
gust the sparrows
off the asphalt

like leaves blown backward.
She wants to know,
Where's their home?

Through the years little changes.
We hope for the best.
We close our books.
We put our heads down
on the desk, down like the lamb.
We make a moment for silence,
make a chamber of ourselves,
our hearts so quiet now,
we can hear the night fathers
struggling to enter.

Ocean Song

In a state of perfect wakefulness
I lie in an upstairs room
of a motel run by Chinese, loving
the sing-song Cantonese
that drifts through the blown windows

above the evening wharves
and the dromedary hills that the shops stagger down,
day curling back into itself
like fog, like dark.
My skin's drawn tight as if upholstered
and burns like sunned leather.

My belly's tender, swollen as an ocean bass,
fatted, asleep, jerking in brackish shallows,
though I know it's just my bladder, festering,
septic, coming now to bump the salt of my groin.

I feed it Cipro and slide the plastic cath,
striped like an immature water-snake,
into the small throat of my penis, wince,
then sigh, and try again to sleep.

Yesterday, a homeless woman, all dog-reek and smoked
hair sat down with me at an outdoor cafe.

She was an ex-M.D. who lived for three years
with a Lakota tribe and cured her ovaries
of cancer when she was finally able to pray
and envision an eagle's claw
pulling the spotted leopard from her womb.

She could see I wasn't ready and would accept
three dollars as admonishment. I don't know,
I think I was. She sang some animal songs for me
and left, sheaves of *The Times* running at her heels,

wind-blown, clasping her calves.

Now the blood refuses music and beats the dull
drum of my head until I shake, until I think
my history, like all history is a diary of battles,
yes, and a pure longing for spring.

I could die here on this field of white
sheets, surprised, just a little,

that it would be all right: to drift this way,
down a marshy estuary, sounding out to the buoys
that mark the harbor channel,
the breathing of deep water.

But the pigeons break from the window's ledge,
swimming up, heavily, past the wake of their clattering.

The door blows open. I rise, fevered, new, almost
unafraid, but soft-shouldering back the odor of dying
fish, that bark of gulls, the bracing air that lives and cools
fire, the whole, frank sea.

After Good and Evil

All these years building a language
for my sorrow then, today, the first

soft rains and the peonies broke open,

without effort. I watched them
in the garden while eating an apple,
slowly, with much relish,

and a certain sadness difficult

to fathom, the flesh, rich and sad
as any animals. I thought, Oh,

I'm becoming a vegetarian,
steaks too rich, fishes stuffed

with my compassion—

all this, since I've been sick. But no,
now the apple giving itself to me,

too, without complaint and I
taking the juiciest bites, unrepentant,
though awed by the need of the world,

circling, all that sadness going round,

a strange and familiar celebration,
and the red, red wonder of it,
dew on my beard, rain,

symbol of loss and great fortune,
even the dusk and the flowers
I may nibble, and the red light
climbing down from the trees.

Retreat

Almost evening,
        under an orange cloud cover
we love one another, attempting
        that slow rasping
erasure of the self
        that fails. Coal-gray stones,
cedar cone with the glow
        of copper, small
carcass of a killdeer, soft
        as a purse, is frost-dipped,
heart-thrust with tiny
        spears of mushroom—the earth
is always gathering.
        It can fill me so much
the trees seem bones
        branching my body.
Here our breath
        calms; the mind spreads
out. Leaves, thin papery
        splotches, fall, yellow and
black, the size of our hands.
        Colors in the beginning
season enter the brain
        secretly; a russet, sedge-wet
grouse flicks pieces of water
        from its wings, stills itself,
disappears, and then the rain
        sweeps in, chilling,
theatrical and dark.
        Your arms, my coat,
become the frail construction
        of our sudden house.
The grasses bend in our direction.
        The wind loves us.
Small animals begin
        their burrowing down,
hard, for a hard winter.

What I See from a Distance

A man in a red pickup lurches along the ditchbank that splits
these fields, covered today, in turn, with light then shadows
of rain. He stops, climbs out and heaves something into
the water and stands there looking after it. What is it
that brings a man this far to give up on something with such
ceremonious disgust? He scans the fireweed that springs
like a belt of stars along the ridge, the clump of alders,
trembling, where I sit, sees me and turns away. The trees lift
with sudden wind, the creeping vines that link their arms
shuddering for a moment. They look like the tiny strands
of lights my neighbors strung last night between the trees
to span the darkness that settled over the wedding there, held
on a patch of new grass and summer flowers. I heard
their daughter say, *I do. I will,* echoed by the shuffling blond
farmhand next to her. And I marveled at their act of faith,
their steady will. My father married young, and the births
that followed seemed to leave him choked with a fear he knew
as anger—a word he whittled down with the wind of his breath
so that it was, finally, swept clean and quiet enough for him.
But, there were signs: an untouched dinner, dull thud of trout
left rank in the sink, or one eye of his that would twitch
like the moths I sometimes stuck with pins. Yet, I remember
a priest praying, making the vague gesture of a cross in the air
above a white box of a size you could use to carry roses
but holding instead my brother, still-borne, and my father looking
off past the parched grass bordering the small aging plots, toward
those few trees sloped down behind the hot metal roofs of a row
of packing houses. I heard a sound come from his throat like pinched
steam escaping a pipe before he turned and walked away. I carry that.
Always it comes back. Today it's in the soft flap of crows rising
behind me, scoffing over the heads of corn, their scattering bodies,
sleek and brilliant in the sun, the pickup, a ball of dust, moving
away in the distance. It was just last night, late, rain smearing
the windows when we lay down, and you wanted from me
what I've never had to give, though I try. How I pressed myself
to you with purpose, though gently, the way a body enters a grave.

Only in the Last Hour

        it is that I watch you,
as if for the first time,
dice Halcyon
with the ritual precision of long habit,
cut moon arcing the window,
cobwebs swelling in wind like blown
glass from the wooden eaves.
        Your eyes fall
to dreaming, tissue of day flowers
collapsing, the soft
        valves of my heart letting the blood
push through with its secret—every road
is a circle. Imperfect
        swimmer, harnessed in a dark, idiot tide
you struggle,
mouth shaping the names
        of lost children, ones you've said
come like shy fish to nudge
your lips open, nuzzle
        salt from your fingers.
This year their faces
appearing in the mail
        swarmed on the refrigerator door
in a collage of your making, accusing us,
as if I were the drunken father
        or you a woman wild
with loss. Yesterday,
lemon-colored leaves
        drifted from the ginkgoes,
sticking to the sidewalks and our jackets
where we walked
        beneath the back-throttled whine of airliners
lifting out of the suburbs, their cargoes

hurtled toward separate futures, a chill
eating at the corners of the afternoon.
I wanted to ask
if it wasn't time for an end
to our checked violence, the chaffing
        of lives drawn too tightly
together, a voice, ringing
like a small bell, clear and cold
in my chest, saying, *Go.*
Then the leaves swirling up,
sulfurous in that light,
        stunning and true.

Holiday

Tide fills the harbor quick as blood in the mouth.
Earlier, I dried my feet and walked away from its voices
breaking on the rocks behind me, sparrows
scuttling like dirty mice along the climbing sidewalks.
Now, in the last hour of service, late afternoon
crowd of students thinning, I drink chocolate,
the waitress clattering dishes into rubber tubs
beneath the counter. She leans her shining forehead
gently to a calendar on the wall
that sports Ohioans skating
ampersands effortlessly under winter maples,
pauses and, as you would when tired,
lifts the bones of her shoulders like a young hawk,
indifferent to anything but the quick
          smoke she's lit and now pulls from
heavily. She sees me and smiles like you
did the first time, her cheeks flushing with something
of the orange in those geraniums burning
in tins of water you painted on the walls of our bedroom.
If you were to take half of everything we own and quit,
          as you said, would you be any richer than the day
you kissed my wrists and fingertips
and said you'd made a false association
between the smell of soaped skin and safety, then laughed
and slipped the wet syllables
of your name into my mouth, though I can't say them
          anymore. Here you
are sliding along the window, more alive than the life
these lines will ever give me, your eyes, dark ink spotting
          paper. The waitress has gone home and I imagine
her washing smoke from her hair, standing
glittering in the shower, relieved to be alone.
You could take the ruby

of blood you left on my lip,
with your handkerchief, take my arm, softly
the way a light wind will sometimes, the way the cold
curls a tentative finger into my sleeve. We could
walk up the avenue together
watching a sky that wobbles above the buildings
with the look of lilacs and ashes, the sharp black
          silhouettes of bare poplars—thin wires the first
warmth will tease into leaf. We could return like old friends,
now brother and sister, to rooms we once slept in,
humbled and quiet, touching the objects there
time has made strange.

The Dreamers

Wind lifts and pivots the marigolds
plunged in flutes of water centering the tables,
plays the strings of the waitress's hair. I wonder
what she'd look like free of that halter—
white pigeons with orange throats, asleep in a Rubens?
With those eyes, a washed, wrung-out blue, she's the picture
of my mother, standing at a window, sometime
in the 60's, rocking her babies, weeping inexplicably
at the sight of old snow spoiled by rain.
That her sense had entered the storm
after too many winters alone was no secret.
I remember her dressing me and my sister
quickly in the dark, hissing prayers of her own
composition, outside skirts of mist resting in the trees.
Where were we going?
Years later, walking a meadow, blood spotted
my sister's thigh like the bright lichen there,
and my mother said, *From now on, girl,*
you keep your legs crossed. Eventually, my sister fled
to the glass-black towers of Chicago, jewel of the corn belt;
a frantic plaintive laugh, too many firemen and accountants,
snow wriggling in off the lakes like a memory.
Sometimes she says it melts before it touches the window.
I like the desert, a hard rain and lightning snapping
the distance, steam twisting from cracks in the ground.
Today, most of the tables are empty.
I cross and uncross my legs and gesture in the air
for more coffee and, I think, against regret.
I watch sparrows lining up in the dusk, topping
an enormous yellow Shell sign buzzing over the avenue,
delivery vans huffing diesel into the gutter.
Sometimes, when a woman walks toward me,
I see how the imagination can tremble into flesh,

and I find myself repeating a phrase like,
The streets run away in darkness
and no one finds us.
Or, sometimes, just
They will be as blossoms laid in a book.
Then I look up; I smile.

New Year's Day, Los Angeles

Watch, sometime, the sparrows,
like worried nuns in their medieval hoods,
collect on the power lines then flee the dusk,
gathering over the shoulders of a town like the one
just passed by the bus you boarded hours ago. See
how night first furs the edges of buildings, then shepherds
each thing completely unto itself. And the lights
tick on, making the sky glow
false in that nearly forgotten and ancient
conspiracy of men to fashion a home out of darkness.
Maybe you, too, would press your face
to the oily window and try to make out those true
constellations, a figure there above, that you might hold
in your arms like a stranger on the eve of this new year
you didn't ask for, and so far from where you began
you don't know it anymore, except by the dull,
congenial letters you sometimes get. Night passes
slowly, and you let go and turn
to the woman sitting next to you, watching.
She's short, plump at the ankles, with the scent
of gin coming off her teeth and little thrift in the sudden,
though expected, kiss
spent on your lips that pull back and smile, too quickly,
and a little ashamed already
of what you will whisper, later, in the welcomed dark
when being alone will no longer seem an issue of grace
or dignity, just a wretchedness
of skin left untouched too long. Later, in the first
pink of the morning, it will be an emblem
of stubborn beauty that will surprise you—her ear,
a curl of potter's clay, little cone of abalone
or a fairy's horn, fallen—just then—empty
and glowing on the pillow. *Mercy,* you'll say,
though you'll know it's not enough.

Note Without Flowers

What you can't grasp—blue flash
        of a jay hopping side to side, featherweight
boxer on the morning sidewalk, bits
        of sun glinting like gold teeth
set high in the little warehouse windows
        fronting the old park, even the tiny,
insistent gnats circling your hand—you'd like to keep.
Light wind grazes your ear. Leaves stir,
        though the trees don't wake,
sunlight stretching its thin membrane

        across the limbs. Though tamed, the geese float out of reach,
honking their brass complaint above the unkempt,
        artificial lake—moss-choked, ditch-brown, more foolish
than sad. Once, here, you watched
        a paramedic, a Puerto Rican girl, sweet in her twenties,
try to blow the wind back into the chilled,
        doll-like face of a tramp who'd drowned, so surely dead
even the crowd fell away, quietly, to leave them there,
        alone, like lovers.

You might have asked what it was that made her
        go on struggling with that failed and heavy dancer,
or why you didn't console her, but you folded
        your curiosity, simply, like the napkin thrust
into the breast pocket of a suit,
        thinned past any real employment.
Now you watch a pair of mockers spin, pecking
the urban crow that hacks a sullen passage west
        beneath a smear of clouds
and know the way this flock of wrens

scatters from an elm, the hours abandon you.
Suppose you asked what it is,
   if anything, that survives...your thoughts climbing
an iron staircase that opens onto roofs and sky, a faint
   day moon, stars that can only be imagined.
You think of women you've touched—
   wind glancing from a frozen pond—and recall
that sharp inhalation they'd make, stilled and alone, their eyes
   looking out at you as into a distance.

Easy

There is a languid certainty
in the way you stretch and then lie down reminding me
of the hawks opening their wings and dropping
from the cottonwoods along the river. This afternoon

when the wind kicked up a dust
and drove evening in and the strange
tom cat showed his bitten face at the window,
you ladled him in with the kind of care one might cup a match.

It was the sort of small and easy thing my mother might have
done when my father wasn't around, brittle with his religion
and anger. You said, *Here, hold him. Easy, dear.*

                    When we were kids, my brother held a match
to the weathered planks of an abandoned barn, and we watched
the flames flick across it like thousands of tiny Koi
wriggling toward the sky, that moist surface that even now
smothers the valley there every winter, and

                    I saw in his eyes that he wanted to be the fire,
perhaps to consume and be consumed
the way everybody in the Bible seemed to me then to be doing.

I recall lying in bed that night wishing I could be a part
of any wild creature that might let me draw near enough

to rough its fur awhile. I was afraid of him
but more afraid because I knew that brothering was,
after all, the hard and necessary part of staying alive.

When we ran across those fields, tethered to the shadows
of our coats flapping behind us, the dry staccato crack

of beams, the whirring heat sucking and exhaling,

I thought it might lift us and could even see in my racing
child's mind, us two rising, like witches I'd read about,

then catching in a tree and hanging
until the birds or maybe possum got at us,
or some rancher in his Ford and sullen curiosity
came by to cut us down.

Once we stood in that very place, rocked back onto our heels,
thrilling at the fact we were
never caught and at that wind at our back, so strong it held us.

        I can see us as if from a distance,
on that hill, laughing. Little fragments

of a laugh roll out from the back of your throat,
        and the smoke you've lit curls and wisps to become
the absence of your voice trailing off and nothing after and how
elegant and simple, how you shake your head at my telling

this and touch my hand, and I'd give anything
not to flinch because I know you're being easy with me,
because you or I might have to go away someday.
Because we will.

The Reconciliation

In the wren's song is its own reason,
inexplicable, somehow holy,
its dull plumage scarcely visible against the bark of an oak
that leafs outside the pane of glass I set last winter
after a small branch stove through.
Only today that singing is insistent
enough to call me outside myself
to offer the small apology of my attention.
Last night my belief in words was shaken.
All that weeping from the other room,
my heart shuffling its solemn two-step,
too quickly, so that I felt my weakness,
truly. Women and their daughters
abide in me always, mysteries
I love. But, sometimes, at the edge of confusion,
I stand as if on hooves of silence, skin-salted, inadequate,
and turn away; I think of my uncle after the war
in Europe, like a mule that moved
only when it wanted, forever dazed
and a little angry, already an old man,
standing in his long coat, gaze
swept out over the diseased field
my father was burning;
untouchable at those times,
I am the boy I was, once, after I found
a dove half-broken, just a dusty scuffle
in red leaves, though the black
oil eyes shone.
I stomped it soundly
so as to let it go. I remember
that in adolescence I told a girl I loved her
because I wanted to know what it was
to live within the warm slip of her kindness,

one wet night in tall grass I can't say I regret,
gathered, held, for a moment
free of myself, then spilled back
into darkness. Today my daughter
hates me because her boy left,
and I lied and said it didn't matter.
When I put my hand on her shoulder
she seemed to shudder and fly away.
This afternoon I am reading Neruda
and seeing him lying in the sun
on the patio of his woman's house,
she inside, asleep and dreaming
petals of soft red arranged round his lips.
It is enough to restore me, because of his surety,
because of his favor, the solace of the ineffable
though ordered assembly of years
that made his mind a bible,
the way he could sever his heart into pieces,
then gently put them where they were needed,
those coins, fishes, the damp nocturnal
embers, a wooden chair draped with quiet
gray trousers. Now beneath this oak
I watch the wren unfist its tentative purchase
in sharp flight, bursting from the limbs,
striking a root to my center.
I must try again, because here,
now, is grace, here is mystery,
my daughter coming toward me,
eyes, watery, and unsure,
here the sun, ladled
even to the low places.

That Year, A Novella

I was already sick when I married and still believed
the doctors could cure me or she would, or all
the inexplicable suffering in the world would
somehow add up in my head which I thought of then,
romantically, as a room like Van Gogh's little attic,
he mad and making there something redemptive.
We'd drive back and forth to Stanford loving the broad
lakes of light on the foothills, tendrils of dark octopus
clouds dragging the distance, some fog always there
and suggesting we were never far from the sea's green
breathing. Still we could laugh until it hurt,
though those years cost us everything. I left school.
She agreed children shouldn't bear the absence a life
of pilgrimage makes. There were times when I'd say
to myself, What's going on? And my self wasn't there
to answer because I was looking into her face that was
one of those fields, and, I, these slivers of dusk falling
into it, and, for a little while, I wasn't scared. When they
severed the muscles of my tongue, stretched and bolted
them to the tip of my jaw, I lay in the back seat as we sliced
home through the mists over Altamont Pass
and thought, It isn't an ear, but I've done it for love,
for the future I didn't know is for everyone a needle's eye
of goodbyes we pass through, the healing, just a long stitching
up that for me didn't work unless dumb animal acceptance
is healing, and I think that it is. So it was right anyway,
and weren't our hearts bells ringing? And the morphine
and wildflowers lighting the skies and the slopes
brilliant blue and that wobbly yellow, a few blackbirds
dropping through, could make me weep at them
and the largess of knowing her and the songs
she hummed, the hope that kept us going back.
It's easy to imagine blood as a betrayal because

it runs easily, but how to show exactly what grew in place
of the lost pieces? All I have to show is the simple fact of her
threading a crowded hospital corridor, eyes that made me
think of blackberries the birds had plucked,
she struggling toward me, my leaking bandage
of a head, her arms full of flowers.

down the stations of the breath...
                                    —Dylan Thomas

Touchstone

Faint waves nose logs stranded along the shore.
        I stop and toe the battered lips of a perch.
                Wind picks at its translucent fins, the sky, close

with the tattered black of a coming front.
        Off a small bluff a sandhill crane catapults, lifts
                and swings around and works its way

along the ridge where maples flame and digger pine
        stretch wide their rusted arms.
                I come again to this boyhood place as the season

starts its great change, the hills
        deepening with bloodied patience.
                I don't know what to ask. Another year

of the dark water that fills my sleep?
        A dog barks somewhere in the trees, faint, persistent.
                The lake twitches like a face as a frog

flays the surface, rippling out, phosphorescent.
        And I think I am not my only father and mother
                as I go each day from breath to breath

in need of a place like this, the charcoal
        reeds, tipped with red, the light that fails softly
                over a cove, these tribes of insects beginning to sing.

All the haunting abstractions slip free and are gone;
and the peace is enormous. —William Everson

The Peace

Between that brief hush before dawn,
        and the morning that comes after,
its sparrows burning
        in the cups of grass,
I hear the wind scurrying
        off the scarred lip of a near ridge, the slow
hurt of it, a pleasure spreading through me;
        I walk out of the cabin I borrow,

built in the 30's, now little more than a pile
        of rock and cedar, to smell the river
blowing up through waterbirch
        and a meadow of bull pine standing, stark
against a dark sky. And I think
        that the loneliness of men is never
wholly answered, unless, perhaps, in lines
        like these...or in the way heat pulls

up a cliff side, abruptly in summer.
        I know below where trees grow, below
the blonde hills that fold in waves
        at the toes of the Sierra,
you sleep, though already
        the summer has turned
your hair the color of tea.
        You're there, and so I am

still anchored to the world. I remember
        last Christmas, driving over Altamont at night,
the white windmills tumbling like acrobats

in the fog, rushing
the throat of the pass and spilling
          inland with me—how strange and
pleasant it was disappearing
          like that, into a cloud. In the afternoons

clouds sweep over, and rain,
          with the long thin legs of a spider,
crawls a horizon of black
          rock and juniper. Sometimes,
I'll stand at the edge of a canyon
          and watch a burst of quail, shot
from the far wall, whistle down
          the years of sediment, circle

and breast the wind, coming to rest
          in clumps of red bud and yucca,
and my mind stops, the way
          fingers of the blind stop
mapping a face in the moment
          of recognition, and the wind
comes down, lifting my hair, and I
          want nothing, then.

MINDY SHORT

D. James Smith's work has appeared in *The Artful Dodge,*
The Quarterly, Stand, The William & Mary Review and many
other journals. A Booklist Top Ten First Novel Pick, a nominee
for the PEN/Faulkner and the National Book Award and a
finalist for The Northern California Book Award, he is the
recipient of The Edgar Allan Poe Award as well as a fellowship in
poetry from The National Endowment for the Arts. He lives in
California's central valley where he studied with Philip Levine.

Notes:

Epigraph with the poem, "Touchstone," is taken from, "Refusal
to Mourn the Death of a Child in a London Fire" by Dylan
Thomas.

The line of William Everson's that appears with "The Peace" is
from his poem, "August."

CPSIA information can be obtained at www.ICGtesting.com
Printed in the USA
LVOW041946050812

293029LV00004B/2/P